Mi A Talk

(I Am Talking)

An Inspired Collection of Poetry with Colouring Pages

Cherry Brown-Graham

Dedication

To my children, Carima, Phylicia, and Patrick Jr.
You continue to be my source of inspiration. You
have added 'colour and flavour' to my life.

Writing has always been one of my passions. There are times when I often find it easier to express my opinions and thoughts in poetic form. These poems were written in different seasons of my life.

Listen

There is something important; we each need to hear
But sometimes, we don't listen simply because of fear;
Fear of what the Spirit may say
Whenever we pray, "Lord, have Your way."
But no matter how long we choose to delay
Or, like Jonah, try to run away,
Like the prodigal son, we must hear and return
To the godly principles, so long we have learned.
We're fearful of the tasks; we think we're unable
However, if you have been chosen, then it's you whom
He'll enable,
The battle is not yours; it is the Lord's
That's the assurance He has given; it's right there in His
words
Quit listening to the negative voices in your head
Just trust in the Lord and go forth instead
Sometimes the bitter pill we'll just have to swallow
So that in sin and condemnation, our fellowman won't
have to wallow.
So, let's open our ears and heed the Spirit's call
Making sure that another soul, without the Word, will
not have to fall.

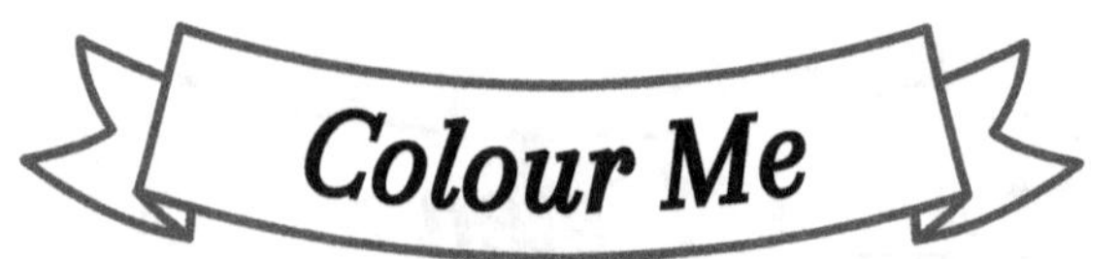
Colour Me

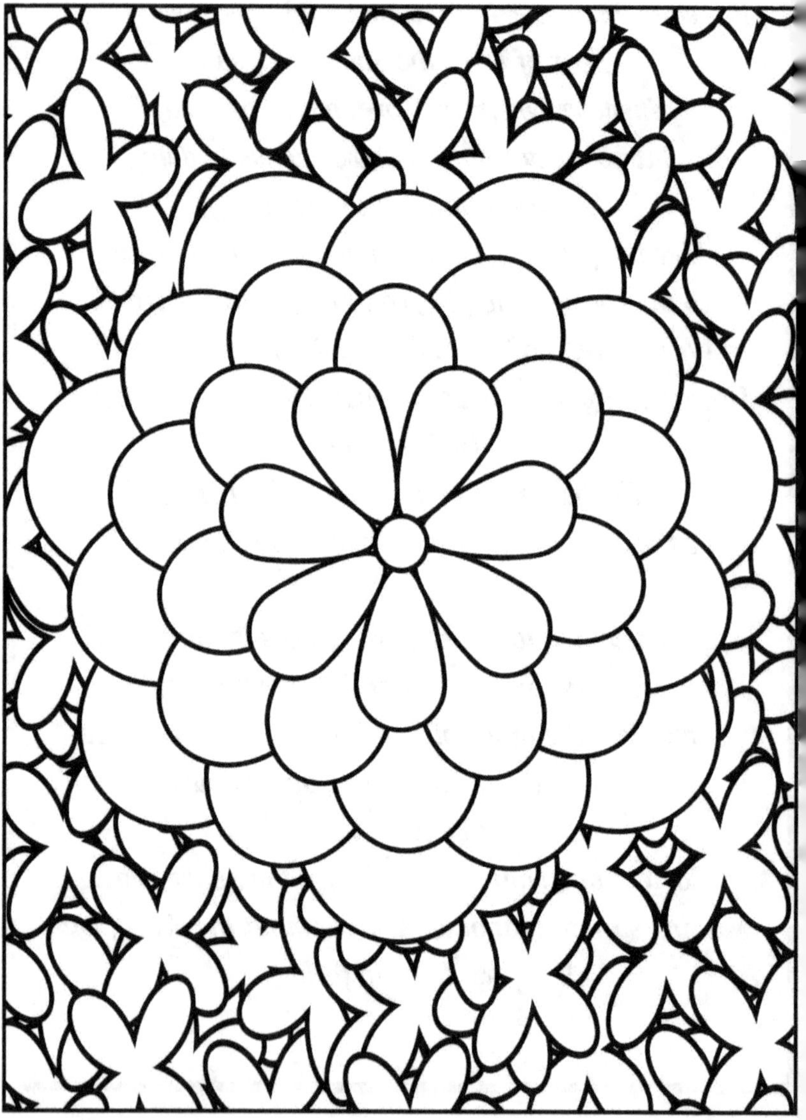

Thankful

*How can I not be thankful for the things You've done for
me? For all the awesomeness, both big and small- even
those I cannot see. You woke me up this morning with
my lungs still filled with breath and kept me throughout
the dark night, far from the chilly hands of death.
Thank You for the air I breathe, the sunshine, and the
rain. Thank You that my body still functions even if
sometimes in pain. Thank You for the table spread with
the water and the bread. For everyone who stretched a
hand, because the Spirit led. Thank You for my family
and friends, acquaintances near and far. Breathe upon
them, Almighty God, You are our Morning Star!
Thank You, great heavenly Father- Jesus Christ, You are
my strength. Thank You for upholding me when my
energy is completely spent.*

*Lord, thank You for Your steadfast love, Your forgiveness,
and Your grace. Thank You for Your faithfulness as I try
to run this race. Nothing that I do or say can adequately
repay. All that You did for me when You went to Calvary
that day. So, as I pen this poem of gratitude to You
I know I'll never have enough words to reflect all You do.
But I pray that as You listen, Lord- You'll help me to stay
true. Until the day I draw my final breath,
I'll forever be thanking You!*

Colour Me

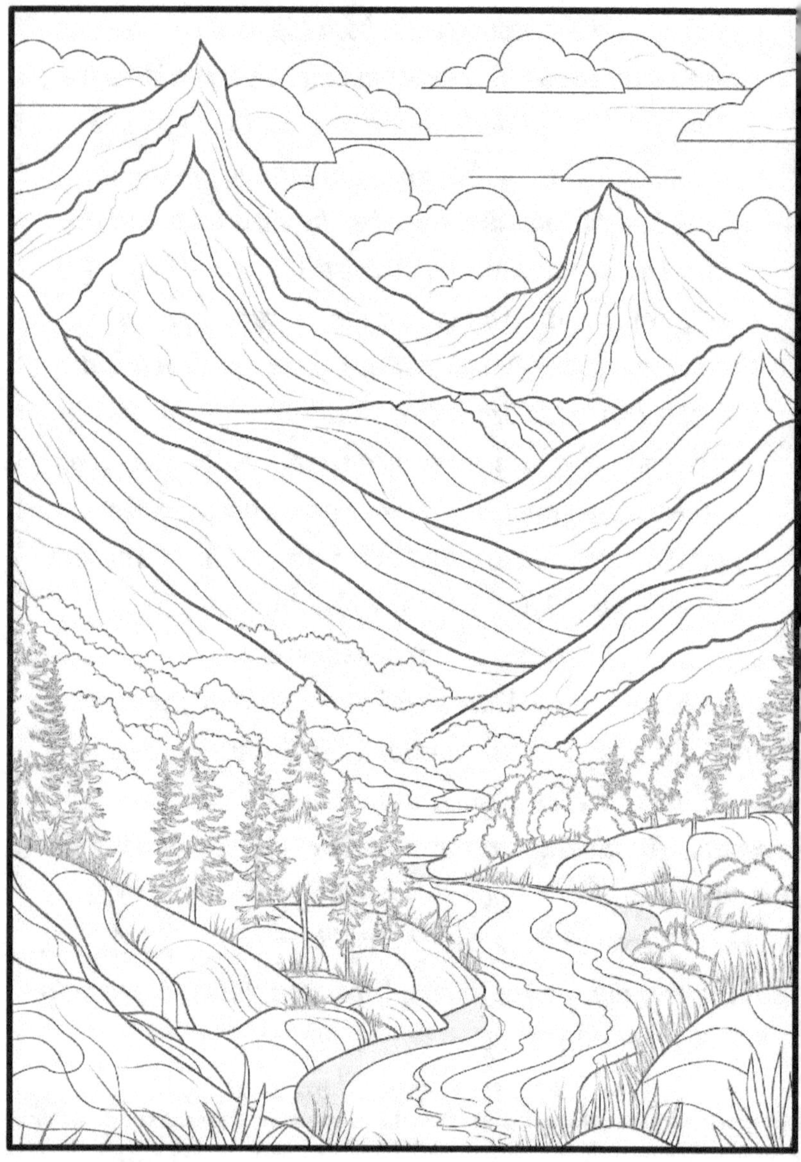

Faithful God

The only reason I tell my story
Is to honour God and bring Him glory
I know that I am not worthy
But that has not stopped Him from blessing me
For every time there was a need
My hungry soul, He would feed
Every tear He would dry
My every need He would supply
O, what a faithful God is He!
Many times, when the way looked dark
And I felt too weary to continue the walk
So dark was the road, so heavy the load
The way I could not see
Yet in those desperate moments, my Saviour carried me
O, what a faithful God is He!
When through the chilly hands of death
A loved one draws the final breath
Our Saviour wraps us in His embrace
And reminds us that the kingdom is a better place
O, what a faithful God is He!

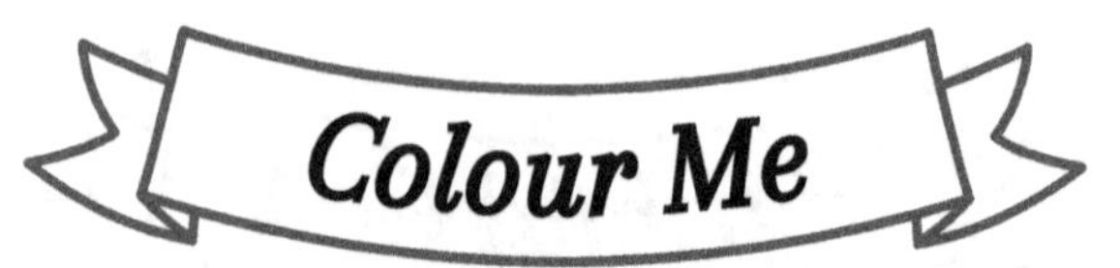

Colour Me

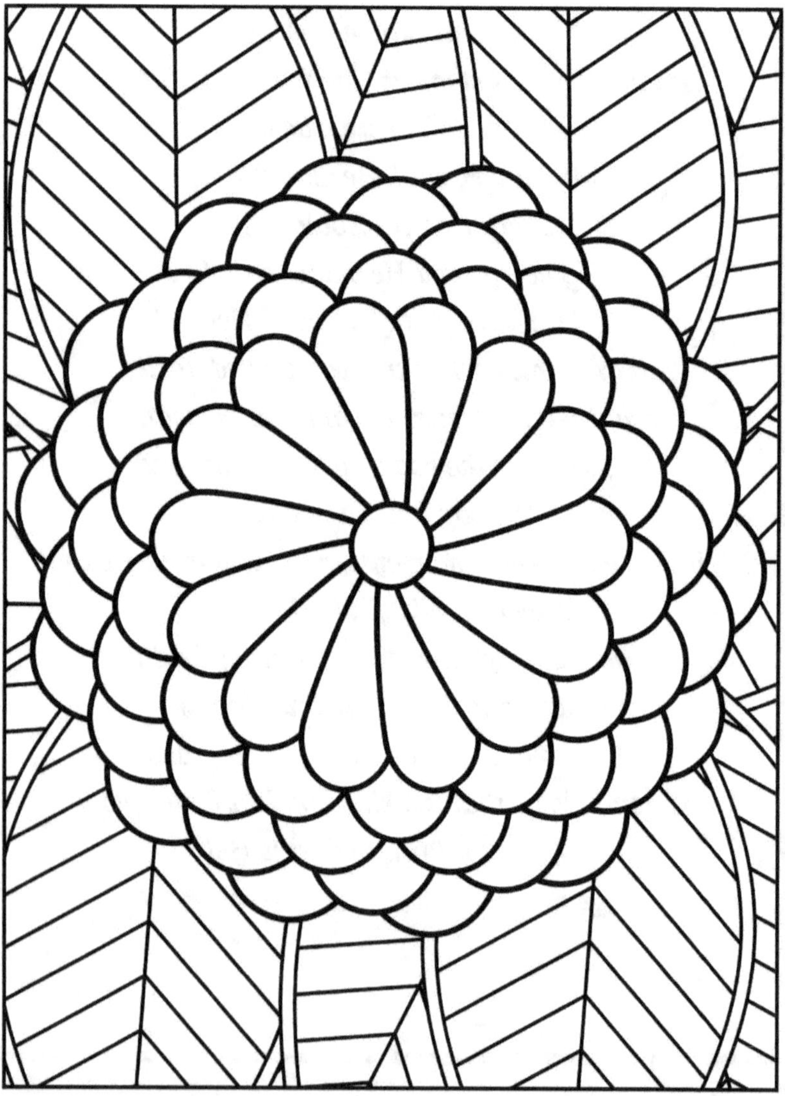

Trust Him

We get up, and we pray every day
Many times, wishing things will go our way
But even Jesus Christ, the only Begotten Son
Prayed, "Father, not my will, but Thine be done."
We often think we're being put to the test
But our heavenly Father knows what's best.
If everything were as easy as we'd want them to be
Then many of us would glorify the 'me.'
Some of the situations we find ourselves in
Are a direct result of the human nature to sin
The scriptures declare that man must repent
If in the New Jerusalem to dwell in his intent
We all have sinned and fallen short of His glory
But praise be to Calvary for the redemption story.
Christ had no sins of His own, yet He was willing to die
To bring eternal life to you and I
So arise from your slumber and get down on your knee
Pray earnestly to Him- say, Lord, forgive me
Your sins will be forgiven, He'll have mercy on thee
In the sea of forgetfulness is where they will be.

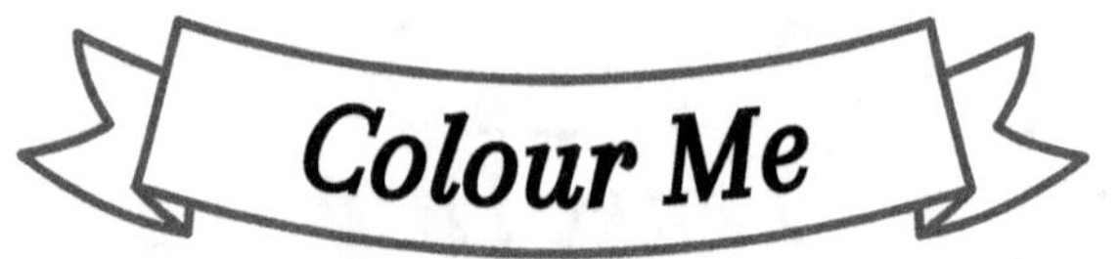

Colour Me

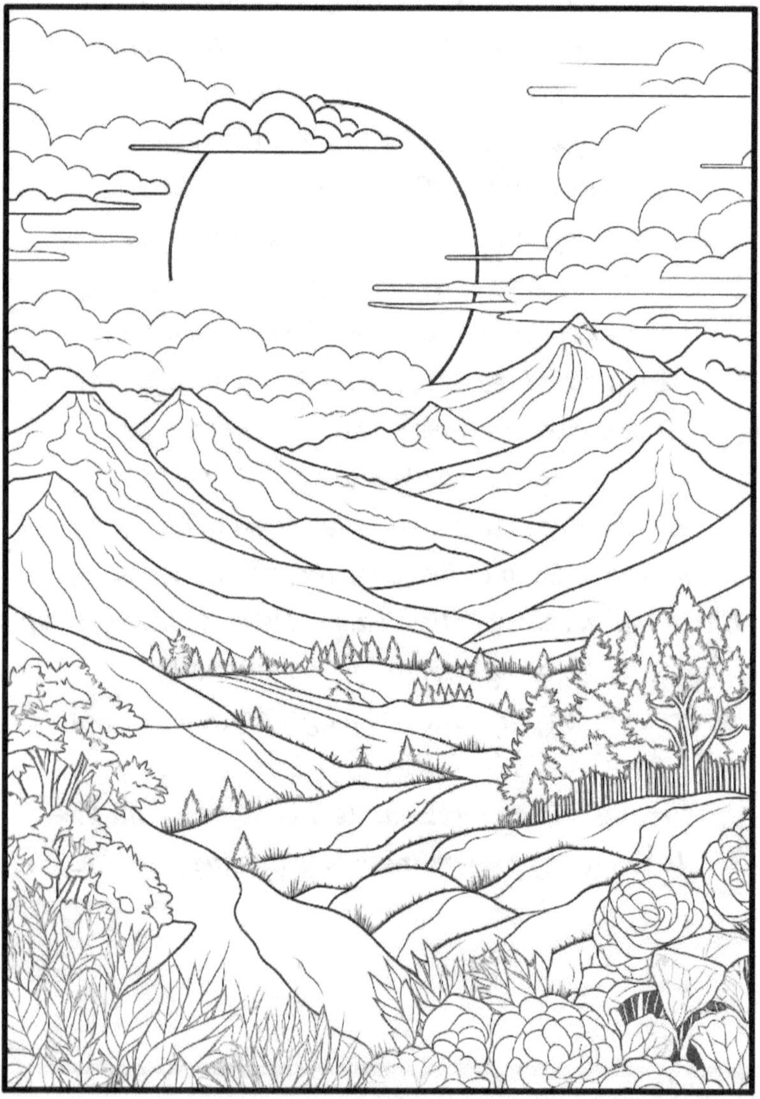

Youths Can Serve

I am here to tell you some truths
About some famous biblical youths
Some may have been younger than you, some even older
The important thing, though, they were all used by the Father.
David was a shepherd boy who slew a giant with a toy
Although Goliath was a giant
Little David crushed him like a pestering ant.
Joseph was a slave and a lowly servant
But to Potiphar's lustful wife, he said, "I can't,
although you are such a flirt, I refuse to lift your pretty skirt."
He was falsely accused, but to sin against his God, he flatly refused.
Have you ever heard of Naaman, the leper?
Well, it was a little servant girl who introduced him to the prophet Elisha.
We don't know much about this little girl
But she knew who was the greatest Healer in the worl'.
Then there was Daniel and his three friends
They were placed in the fire, he in the lions' den
To the golden statue, they did not bow
And refused to eat idol worship chow.....

...*Now I want you to picture this,*
Five peg bread and two 'likkle' fish
Was what a small boy had in a lunch dish
But Jesus gave thanks and then blessed the food
And with it, the disciples fed a whole multitude.

So, don't mind your age, your gender, or size
You serve a purpose in God's eyes
Like Timothy said in the 'Book of Truth.'
"Let no one despise your youth."

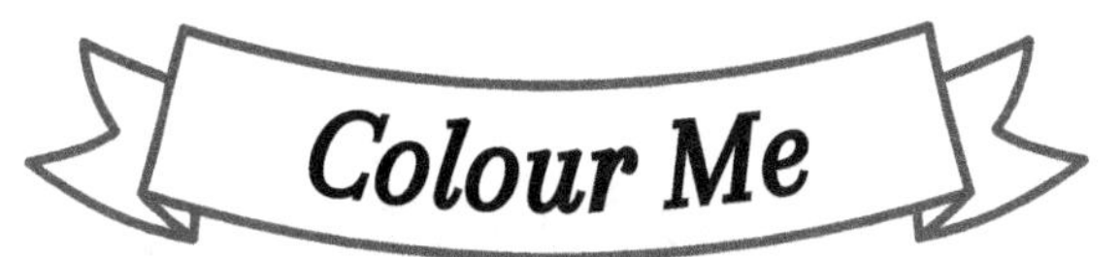

Colour Me

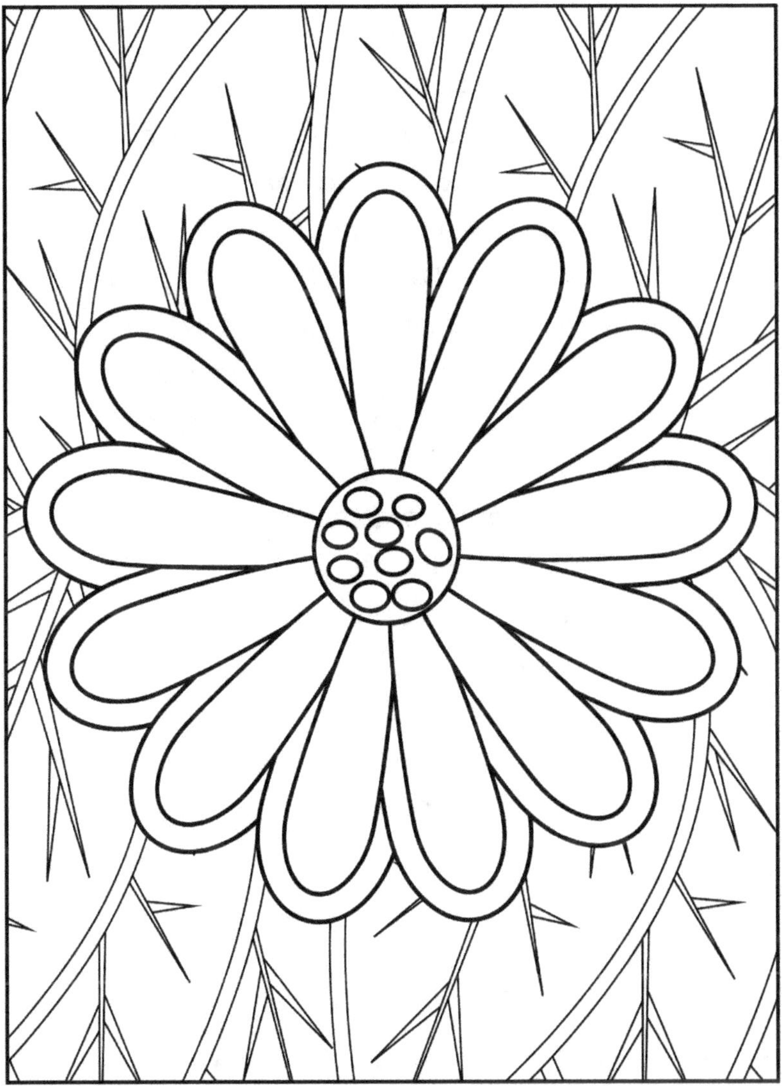

Tick Tock!

...Do you know what time it is?
Don't look at the clock,
No! Don't look at your watch.
Have you been counting the moments?
Or have you been making your moments count?
It is said that we hatch, match, and dispatch
But in between, shouldn't we all make an impact?
Never underestimate the little you can do
Touch a life positively before bidding this life adieu
You never can tell who you may inspire
By as simple an act as lighting a small 'fire.'
The warmth or light you emit
Could be just what is needed
To save someone from the pit.
So, as of today, while on your way
Instead of dying for the day to end
Spend the time living so that you and others will live
again.

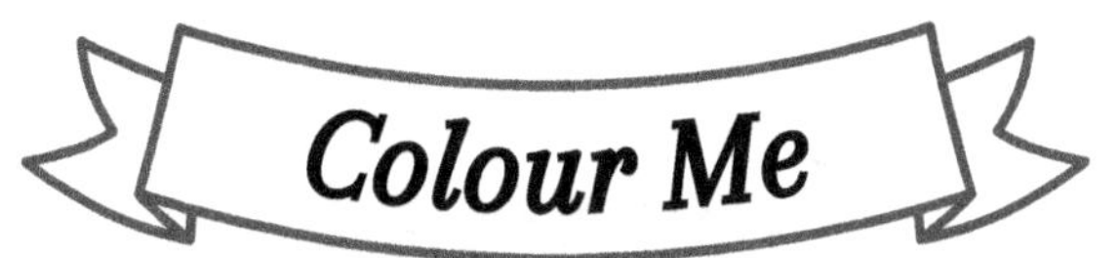
Colour Me

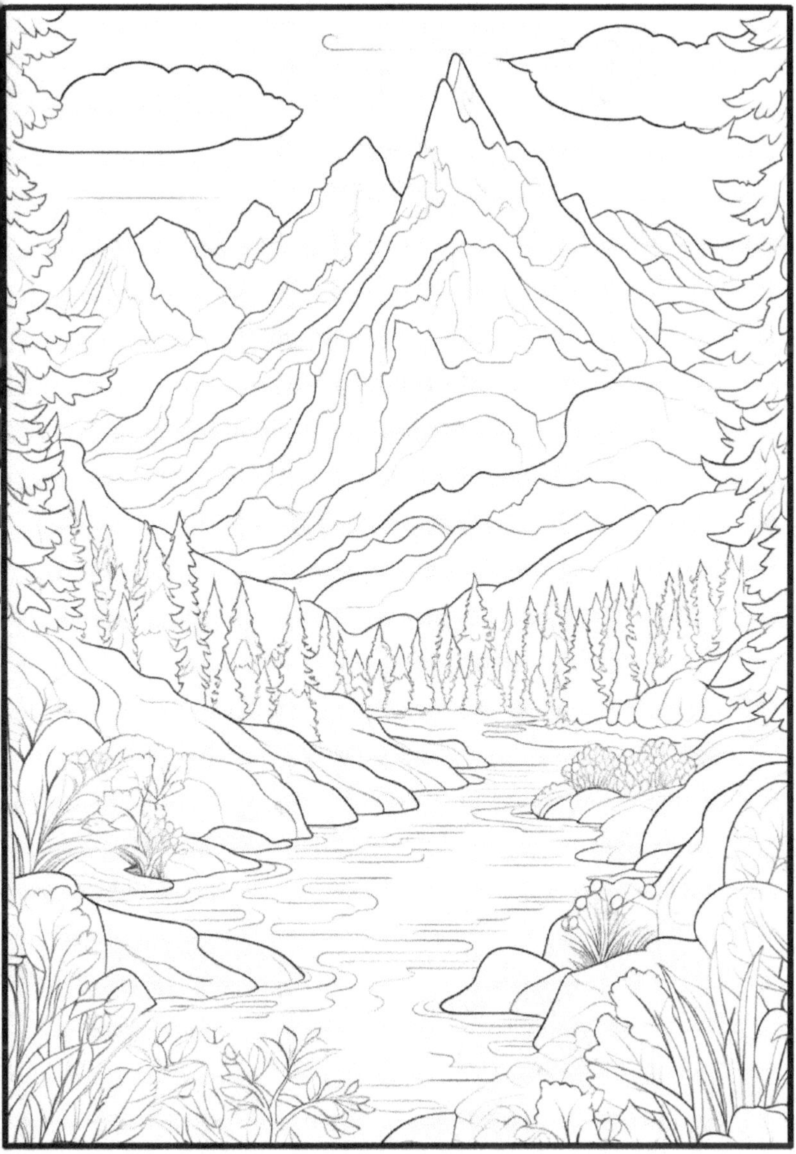

Cheerleader

Not everything you hear, you should believe
Some people's aim is to trick and deceive
They try to twist you up with their lies
And seemingly authentic alibis
When in truth and in fact
The only intention is to stab you in the back.
Don't listen to their excuses
They know what abuse is
That's only a ploy,
Your life they aim to destroy.
Do you hear them applaud?
Now, there goes the fraud!
Learn to cheer yourself on.
Everyone else will soon be gone.
Practice self-love,
Seek approval from above
Compete with yourself,
Reach for the top shelf
Set high expectations,
Move forward with determination
Trust your Creator and know that sooner or later
If in yourself you believe
All your goals you'll achieve.

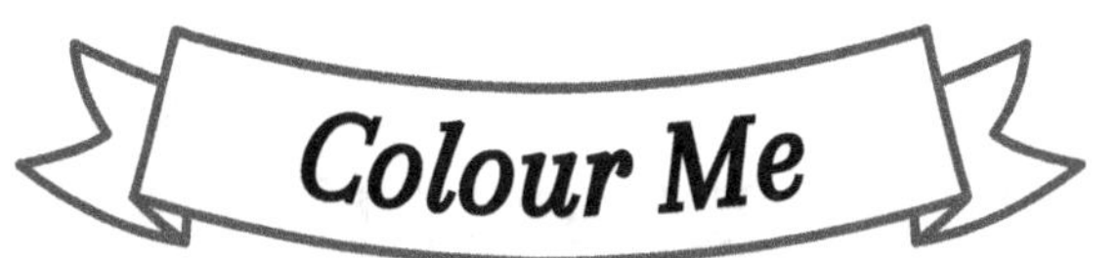
Colour Me

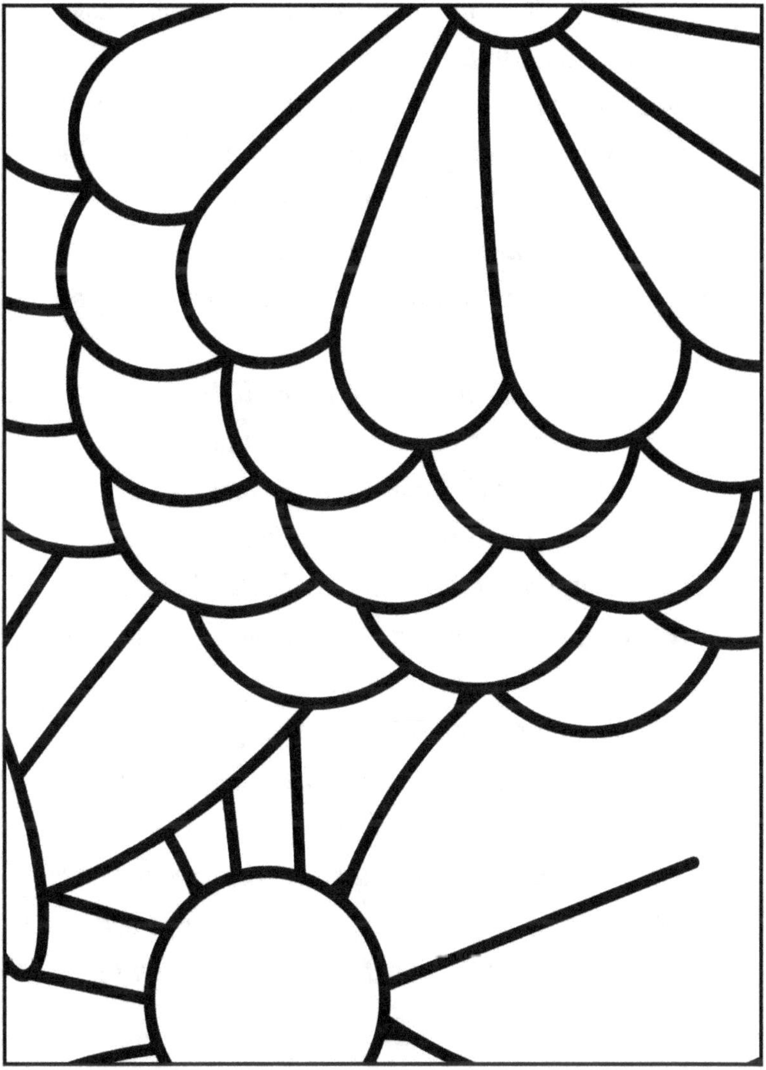

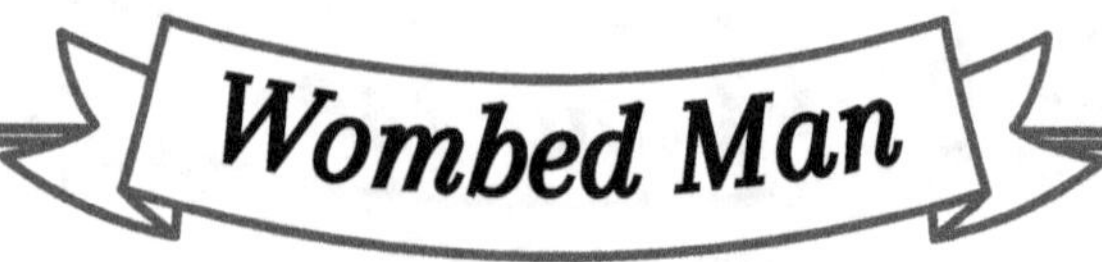

Woman- this man with a womb
Created by God to be a helpmate to whom?
Could it be the same man from whom such abuse
Is meted out to with some flimsy excuse!
She was created to be a mother, daughter, sister, or wife
Not for some heartless creature to snuff out her life.
From the beginning of time
She's told, "Toe the line."
Yet in every major achievement, her contribution you'll
find.
Don't breastfeed in public!
Obey your man and be quiet!
How much longer can we survive
On this restrictive diet?
You say our suggestions make absolutely no sense
But when faced with a challenge, they become your
defense.
We do what we do with the best of intentions
Because we're aware that we're the nurturers of future
generations
We don't want to be treated better than we deserve
We're willing to assist you; we're willing to serve,
But treat us as equals give us respect, trust, and love...

...Keep your hands to yourself
Or put on your silk glove
So that when next you touch her
It will be to caress her
And let her know that you think you are blessed
That you are the one who caught her interest!

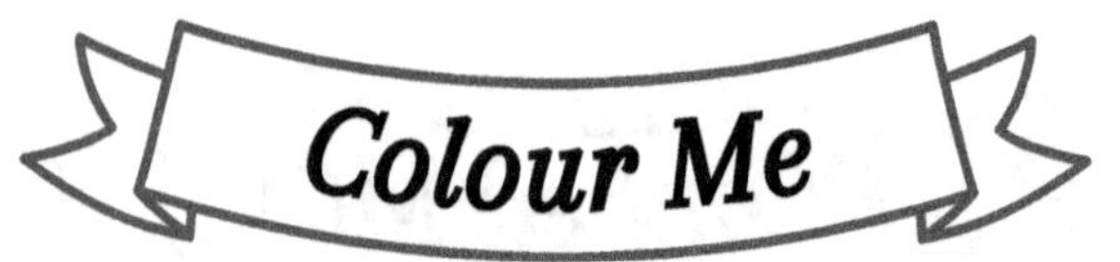
Colour Me

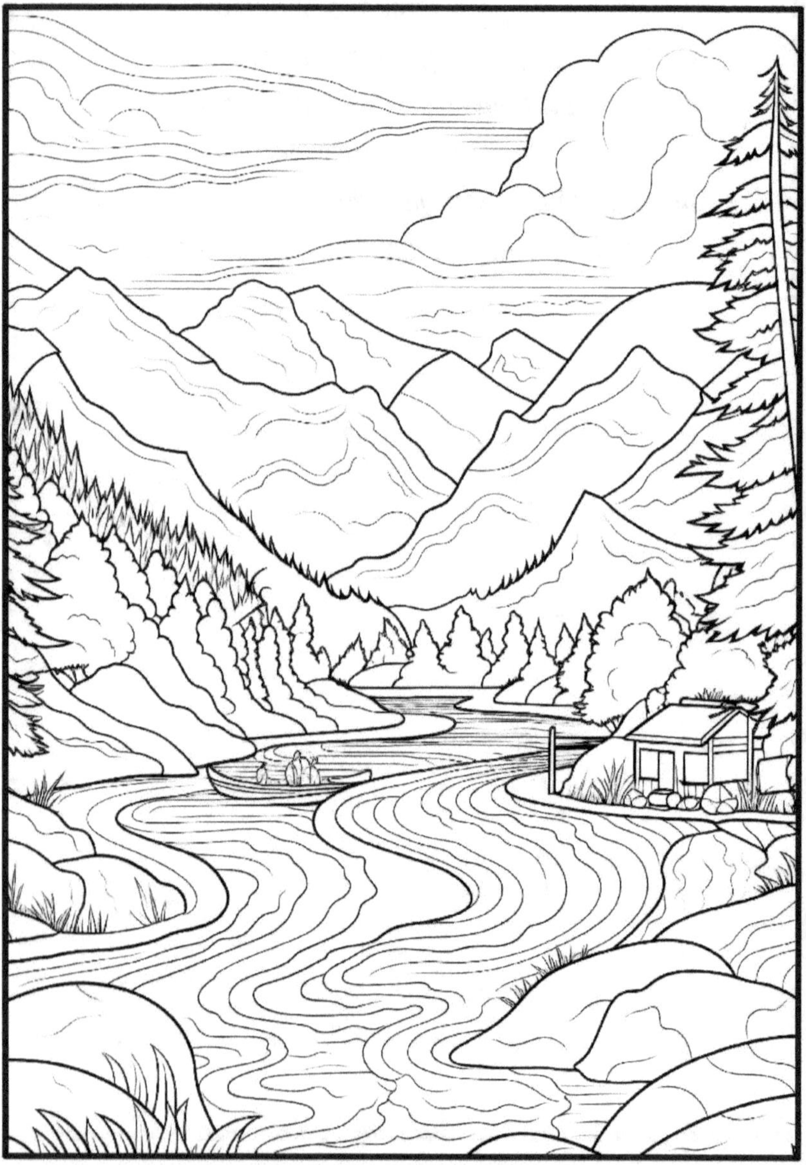

Melanin Pride

If every time you look at my face
The only thing you see is my race
Then it is you who are blind
The one civilization has left behind.
This black skin I am wrapped in is no greater a sin
Than that pale one that you are in.
When God created me, you see
He placed within my destiny
How dare you think you are the one
Who should decide the end of me?
The extra melanin that's in my skin
Is a reflection of my strength within
I wear this hue with pride and joy
Though the majority of you it seem to annoy.
Throughout history, you've used my strength
To increase your wealth to a vast extent
Collectively, our blood, sweat and tears
Have enriched your coffers down through the years
Despite the hardships we've endured
On wings of love, we'll continue to soar
So, though you're intimidated by the colour of my skin,
My greatest strength really lies deep within.

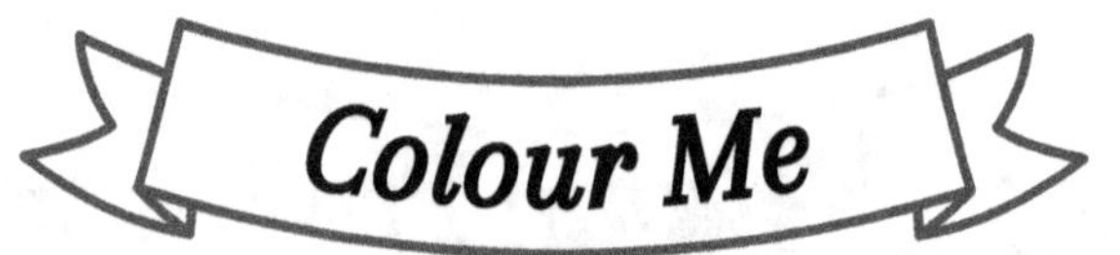
Colour Me

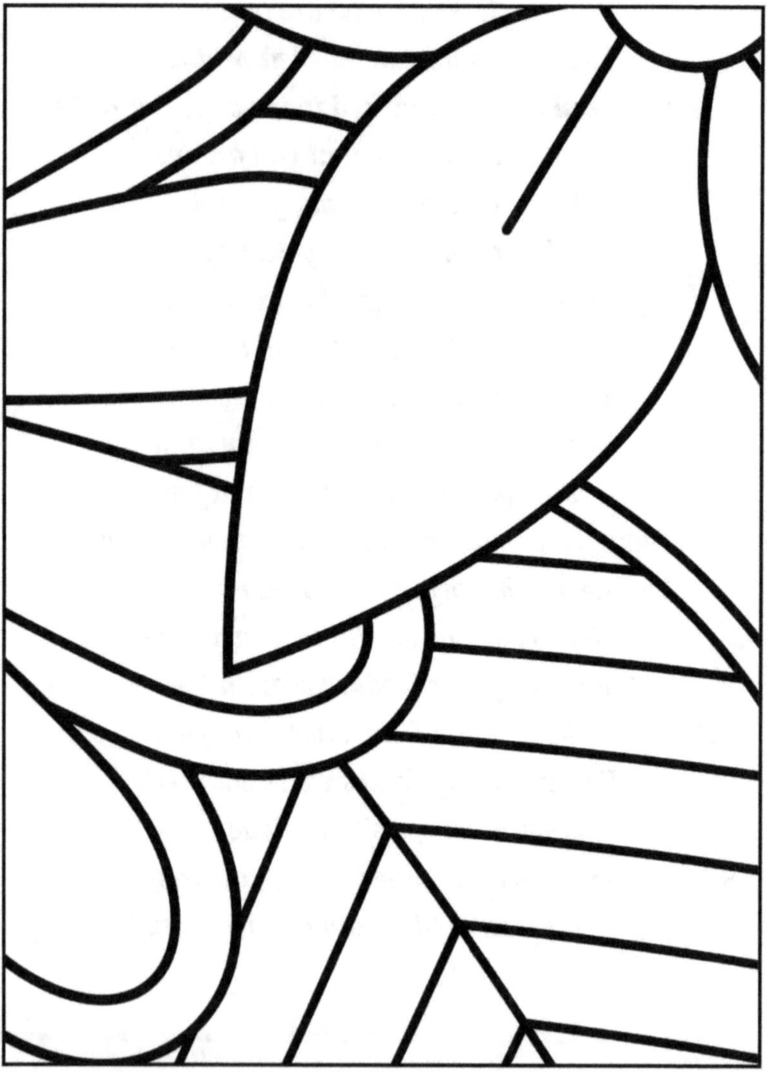

Warriah!

Unnuh seh mi is a Obeah ooman
A jus tru unnuh nuh undastan mi man
When dem teck mi from Ghana carry come yah
Dem neva know seh mi was a warriah.
Teck me outta mi nice comfat zone
An a neva jus mi alone
Dem teck mi an mi Breddah dem
Fi come wuk wi out like wi a dem fren
Pack wi inna ship battam like wi a sardine
Like seh dem nuh know seh wi have feelin.
Is not dat mi did fraid fi hard work
Mi just neva plan fi dweet fi nuh ole jerk.
How mi fi werk when yuh a beat mi?
To mi, dat a real hypocrisy
Yuh siddung inna shady every chance yuh get
An yuh nuh waan mi fi tap fi even wipe sweat.
So call mi obeah ooman if yuh want
Mi nah siddung inna slavery when mi can chant
For when mi an my African Breddah an Sistah dem
waan to guh free
Yuh an di whole a yuh wicked fren dem goin have to
flee.

Colour Me

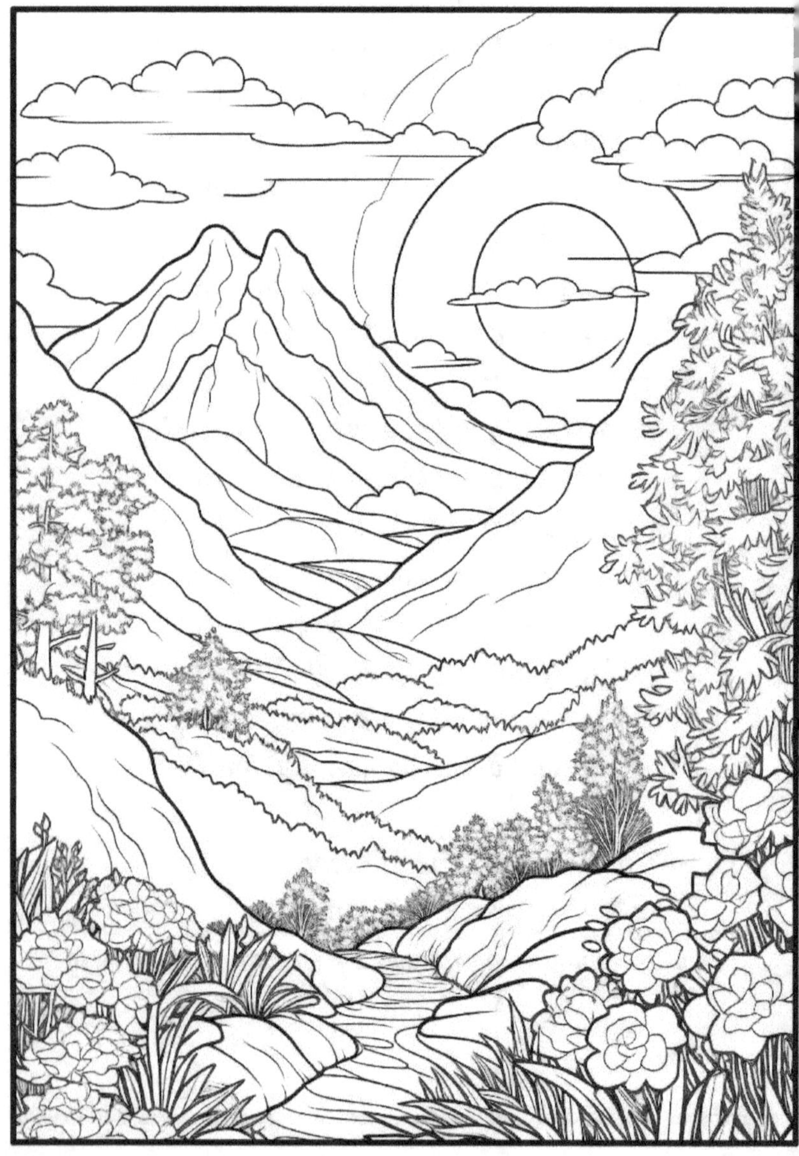

Not Yet!

Whose is the most important voice in your head?
What do you first hear when you roll out of bed?
Of all those little voices that you always hear,
Which do you listen to, do you even care?
There's always a still, small voice speaking to you
Telling you all those things you have to get through,
Sometimes you rush, and you fuss, and you try to decide
How many of these chores can I really avoid?
So you start getting things done and begin to get flustered
And suddenly realize not a "Thank You" was muttered
You stop for a while and slow the pace down
Look up to the Father and say, "God, I'm Your own
Help me to get through this day with its tasks
And forgive me for starting before Your permission I'd asked.
In my moment of weakness, I'd forgotten You see,
That the strength that I need is found only in Thee
So please give me the strength to go through this day
And help a lost neighbour who knows not the way
May my life be a light that shines brightly each day
To brighten the pathway for someone going astray
Lord, each day that I wake up
May I never forget
That I'm only awake because You whispered, "Not Yet!"

Colour Me

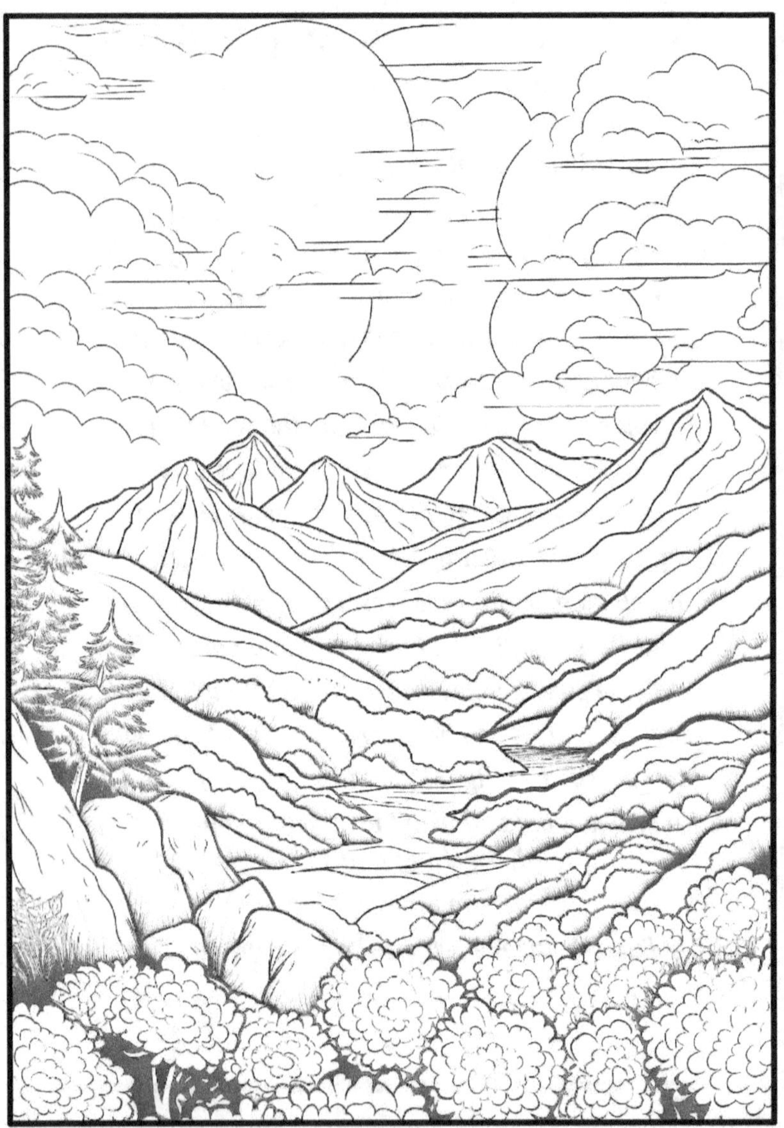

Acknowledgement

To my heavenly Father for His presence, which has guided me, His love, which has strengthened, and His voice, which continues to whisper encouragement even in my moments of doubt.

To my friends, especially Charmaine, Pauline, and Pearl Lyn, who have always told me that there's a book somewhere inside of me.

Most importantly, to my children for their unconditional love, support, and belief in me.

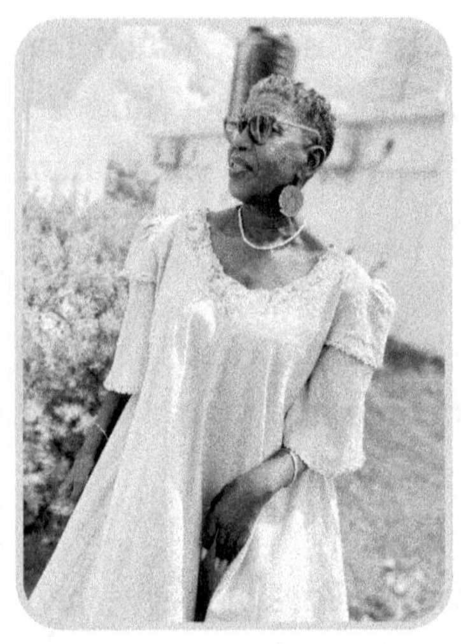

Cherry Brown-Graham is a Retired Teacher, Trained Guidance Counselor, and a member of the Board of Elders at Salem United Church (United Church in Jamaica and the Cayman Islands. She is a mother of three adult children (two daughters and a son).

Cherry is actively involved in Church and community activities and is passionate about the welfare of children.

www.ingramcontent.com/pod-product-compliance
Lightning Source LLC
Chambersburg PA
CBHW050624160726
48003CB00003B/1322